Dave LaRue

LIVE TO TELL YOUR STORY

STORIES AND DECISIONS ON THE ROAD TO SUCCESS

The opinions expressed in this manuscript are solely the opinions of the author and do not represent the opinions or thoughts of the publisher. The author has represented and warranted full ownership and/or legal right to publish all the materials in this book.

Live to Tell Your Story
Stories and Decisions on the Road to Success
All Rights Reserved.
Copyright © 2012 Dave LaRue
v2.0 r1.0

This book may not be reproduced, transmitted, or stored in whole or in part by any means, including graphic, electronic, or mechanical without the express written consent of the publisher except in the case of brief quotations embodied in critical articles and reviews.

Paperback ISBN: 978-0-578-10854-4
Hardback ISBN: 978-0-578-10861-2

Library of Congress Control Number: 2012914640

The Genius Platform Publishing Company

PRINTED IN THE UNITED STATES OF AMERICA

Acknowledgments

I believe that relationships are one of the best parts of life and I would like to acknowledge everyone who has been a part of my life as I gathered these stories, and everyone who played a part in the stories themselves: my family, friends, business partners, and the teams at my companies. Thank you.

Thanks to Dan Sullivan, Babs Smith, and the team at Strategic Coach for helping me to embrace my unique ability, and for giving me the opportunity to share it for the last fourteen years.

Thanks to my editor, Robert Klein.

The book is dedicated to my grandson, Luke David LaRue

D.L.

Introduction

What you see here is not the first attempt I've made at writing a book.

At first, simply enough, I planned to put in print the concepts and methods that had I found to be most helpful to my coaching clients; to share the principles and processes that I had seen transform the thinking of so many people and ultimately change their lives.

But the more I worked on writing a book like that, the more I started thinking about how many books had already been written in the last one hundred years, and how few people had used these books to their full potential. Why was that? How could my book be any different?

The answer was clear when I started thinking about the difference between writing a book and coaching an individual in person. What I recognized is that in person, I'm having a conversation with someone, getting instantaneous feedback about whether the language I'm using is working, and I can change it on the spot if my language isn't communicating effectively with that particular person.

I had to adjust my thinking accordingly.

Since I wasn't going to be able to custom-tailor the way I explained something once it was printed, instead of using a set of specific terms to communicate an abstract concept, I would just do what comes naturally: tell a story.

By telling a personal story and then linking it up to the lessons that I learned from it, I could communicate the concepts I wanted to share, while the story's resonance with each reader's own life made it possible to apply the concepts to their lives, and, even better, to start thinking about their own stories and extracting their own lessons from them in a personal and powerful way.

While we're all aware of how effective stories are as a tool for learning—parables, proverbs, jokes, and so on—what's been missing from the literature is the lesson *about* all these lessons: something happens when events in an individual's life are arranged in a story. Something about the process transforms a list of facts or memories into a tool for gaining true understanding about a situation and, more deeply, for communicating something about what each person's life is about in a way that they can reflect on or share.

Stories have a point—a lesson, a meaning. Finding meaning in our lives is one of the deepest elements of true success. I believe that each of us has a great storehouse of wisdom waiting to be explored in the stories of our lives. By sharing the stories that have taught me the most, I hope not only to share those stories and lessons with you to use as you see fit, to use for yourself or to share with someone else in your life, but to encourage you to look at the events and relationships in your life—your victories and your challenges, your dilemmas and compromises, your friends, family, mentors, and rivals—as each being a story, each with a lesson that informs and prepares you to make the best decisions you can as you chart and navigate your path to success in life.

Storytelling is perhaps our oldest tradition, and one of the human realities of telling stories is that the listener, as they listen, often finds themselves thinking about the stories from their own life that relate to what they're hearing—sometimes the relation is surprisingly close; sometimes it's only a loose association. Whatever the case, bringing the stories of your life into focus as you read the stories in this book is a large part of why it was written.

Here are my stories.

Contents

Acknowledgments	iii
Introduction	v
Playtime in South Dakota	1
Good Morning	3
Look at the Trucks	4
Shoes Shined	7
Pass the Ketchup	12
The Man on the Airplane	18
"Can't You Just Lie to Me a Little Bit?"	21
Life's Defining Moments	26
Goalie Days	31
Trophies	35
The Teacher Appears	38
Not Everyone Will Be Coming With You	43
Giving	48
Understudy to the Prodigal Son	51
Afterword	58

Playtime in South Dakota

When you're able to do what you love the most and what comes most naturally to you, communication feels effortless. Ideas and information flow freely among everyone involved. Because of this, it is the most productive way to work. Not only that, it *feels good*. It's enjoyable. You want to do it as much as possible. It feels like playing. So the phrase I can't help but use when I'm asking people to get into the frame of mind necessary to work with me when I'm leading a team or coaching is "Play with me."

One time, I was doing a workshop for a group of entrepreneurs in South Dakota. They were all stern-looking guys, many wearing Western gear. I was wrapping up my opening speech and I said, "Okay, are you ready to play with me?" They didn't expect to hear that. They looked around and asked each other, "Did this guy just ask us to play with him?"

When I'm leading or coaching, I'm in my playground. I love helping people set their goals. I love to ask questions and motivate you to live your life. If you have a desire to work on yourself, a desire to learn more tools to do it, if you're ready to play, then we can do this. If you don't do this for yourself, if you don't take charge of your own life, who will?

Working on yourself doesn't have to be a chore, and it certainly won't work well if it's something you find displeasure in. There may be some uncomfortable truths you'd rather not address. It may be surprising to see the habits you need to change and the new ones you'll have to cultivate, but making the adjustments you need to make to become the person you really want to be is a purely positive process. It's something everyone has an ability to do, and once you allow yourself to be open to it, learning lessons and making changes in order to achieve results is one of the most rewarding activities in life.

So let's play. Ask yourself: What do you want in your world? Who do you want in your world? As you look around and notice what or who is or isn't in your life right now, realize—it's up to you.

It's all up to you.

Are you ready to play?

Good Morning

Good Morning

This is what I think to myself when I wake up in the morning:

"This is the beginning of a new day. I have been given this new day to do as I wish. This day is important to me because I'm exchanging a day of my life for whatever happens in it. When tomorrow comes, this day will be gone forever, leaving in its place something that I have traded for it. I want that something to be:

Health; harmony and love; meaningful, joyful relationships; being authentic and real; freedom and the opportunity to create freedom for others; wealth; finding opportunities for myself and others; having great opportunities to coach and to lead my companies; great travel experiences and experiences with others; and wonderful stories.

All of this in order that I shall not regret the price I paid for today, that being a day of my life.

What's your "good morning" thought?

Look at the Trucks

Like many people, I was not blessed with an ideal childhood.

I had a speech impediment that caused me to pronounce my T's as F's. I made heads turn when I said something like, "Hey, look at the trucks." To make matters worse, I wet the bed at night, which was an ongoing source of embarrassment and shame. When I walked the halls at school, I felt there was a sign hanging from my neck that said, "Another Wet Night—What a Loser!" I grew up with an alcoholic father who spent most of his time in an intoxicated state. His destructive, repulsive behavior ruled our house. His physical abuse toward my mother, my sister, and me kept us in a constant state of fear, and his verbal abuse beat down my self-confidence. I had constant anxiety from the fear that my drunken dad would show up at school or sporting events, and show his true colors. As if all this were not bad enough, an ulcer was beginning to form in my stomach.

Dignity did not seem to be my destiny when I was a young boy. I remember that feeling like it was yesterday.

But I also remember the moments when things changed.

One of the most significant turning points in my childhood was when I was ten years old and I tried out for the Little League majors. I made the team. I was one out of only two ten-year-olds selected to play on the team, and the pride of accomplishment that I felt was a boost to my self-confidence that I hadn't expected.

As I started the baseball season, my coach, Coach Butner, must have had insight into my situation. He put his hand on my shoulder and said, "Young boy, you're a good person and a good player. You are going to be okay. I'll help you be all that you can be." I didn't realize it at the time, but that moment changed my life. In your daily life you may not think much about the impact that you are having on someone, but you are having an effect. Sometimes it may be life-changing.

When I became an adult and I started to reflect on my past and determine what I wanted my future to be, I recognized how powerful Coach Butner's statement was, and how much it truly shaped me. He was instrumental in putting me on the path to accomplishing great things. He inspired me to believe in myself and gave me the gift of knowing that just as he influenced my life, I could influence the lives of others.

Another powerful moment of change was when my mother and I moved out of the house. Even though we lived in her car for six weeks, they were the happiest days of my life. I felt free and safe. Free to now have a good life. I was not going to screw it up. I made a vow to myself that my life would be better and I would make conscious choices throughout my life to ensure that I would not be in a destructive environment again.

I find it especially powerful to think about how much you can change your life in a single day. The day my mother and I moved out of the house marked the start of a brand-new life for both of us. From that day forward I began to take note of what defined success in life. With little to no support at home to teach me about how to achieve success, I had a lot to learn. By my late teens, I was reading every book about personal development and personal growth that I could find. I began to put myself in situations where I could meet and network with successful people. I wanted to learn from people that had already achieved success. I studied the habits of productive people and the habits of unproductive people. With the understanding that we are the creator of our habits, I began to incorporate success-cultivating habits into my life.

I don't dwell on the past, but I don't deny it, either. When it comes up, I find that reflecting on it can provide me with clarity and the extra motivation to make my life better. I can remember moments that proved how powerful and possible change is, even in situations that seemed hopeless. Based on people I've known, I suspect that a large majority of true entrepreneurs have similarly impactful beginnings to their timelines, and from that, a personal treasury of experiences like this to draw from.

Look at the trucks.

Shoes Shined

Bob Nyrop was a major figure in my life. He was my mentor, friend, business associate, father in-law, and my boss. He was like a father to me. He shared his values and taught me countless lessons. He was an inspiration to many people that he met, and there's one story about him that was shared with me at the end of his life, which I'd like to share now.

We were well into the second year in a tense lawsuit when Bob was deposed by a law firm that was notorious for going for the kill no matter what their case was. Part of their overkill strategy was that they deposed Nyrop intensely for two days. The deposition generated 317 pages of questions and answers.

Less than two weeks later he suffered an aortic aneurism. The lawsuit went on despite this.

During that time my days would start by being at the hospital by 6:00 a.m. I would stay until at least 10:00, then, when the doctor would come, I'd leave for a few hours and head over to my office at Baldwin for the next several hours trying to cram as much work as I could before heading back to the hospital.

The odds are that most people in the same situation would not survive beyond a couple of hours, but Nyrop hung on. He managed to fight for twenty-one days with the best efforts of his doctors, who performed fourteen different procedures, and a lot of hope and prayers from his family.

When Nyrop passed away I was devastated. I felt scared and lost. When he died I lost the one person that accepted me for me, something that I appreciated at the time, but something that means even more to me now.

The planning of the funeral was very tense and extremely sad. I was trying to be strong for my family, but inside I was going through so much turmoil. On the day of the funeral, I just really wanted to be able to get through, but instead of the funeral being a purely sad event, Nyrop had one more lesson for me.

In testament to the many lives that Nyrop touched, there were over 800 people in attendance at his funeral. I stood up at the casket near the altar before the funeral service. I was one of two men standing there with our heads solemnly bowed down. I glanced up and was surprised to see that the man next to me was Steve, our company insurance rep. He was crying as hard, if not harder, than me, but even as emotional as the day was, I couldn't help but notice how professional he looked. His suit was immaculate. His shoes were spotless. The service started and we had to take our seats.

I remember thinking throughout the service about Steve standing there crying with me. I think about 400 or so people stayed for the typical Minnesotan/Lutheran reception, complete with goulash, potato salad, Jell-O, and dessert bars. I searched the room looking for Steve. I had to know his story—why was he crying so hard about losing someone he just sold insurance to?

Steve explained with a story and that was one more lesson Nyrop left for me.

Steve told me that his first job after graduating from college was with an insurance company, and his very first call was on Baldwin Supply Company with Bob Nyrop. Steve was competing with several different agencies and worked hard on getting the business, meeting with Nyrop several different times.

Decision day finally came and Steve had his meeting scheduled with Nyrop. He got to the office fifteen minutes early, and sat in the lobby nervously waiting to be called back to Bob's office. He was feeling confident about getting the account, but still wasn't 100% sure. It would be his first deal. He said he was clammy and almost shaking because he was so nervous.

Then the moment came. Nyrop called him into his office and after a few minutes of small talk, Nyrop said, "Steve, I'm impressed with the results you've gotten, your responsiveness, pricing...." Then the old man went silent for about 10-15 seconds. Steve said it felt like forever and he just froze.

Nyrop got up from his chair and closed the office door. Then he sat down on the chair next to Steve and said, "Steve, I really want to give you our business. You've worked hard for it and you deserve it." Then another 15 seconds of silence. Steve thought in those moments that he had lost the account.

Nyrop looked down at Steve's shoes and continued, "But, if you treat our business the way that you treat your shoes, I'm afraid that you won't provide us with the level of service that we expect. You see, it's one thing to get the business, but it's another to maintain the business. The condition of your shoes tells me that you'll just go out and buy a new pair next year... just like maybe you will just go get another account if we don't renew with you.

"If you want to be successful, you need to display that you care; that you are going to maintain what you have; that you protect your investments. You need to shine your shoes, son. You need to demonstrate that you care, and that you can and will make sure to serve our business better than any of your competitors could. You have all of the ingredients to be successful: your presence, intelligence, energy, likability... but you won't get the opportunity to do business with us if I'm concerned that you don't take care of your stuff."

Apparently Nyrop and Steve came to an understanding at that point, because the old man took a chance and gave him the account that day. Steve has gone on to become one of the top performers for his company for over thirty years. Every time you run into Steve, his shoes are shined. On the day of Bob's funeral, he shined his shoes to where you could almost see your reflection. This was Steve's way of showing his respect to the man that taught him one of life's greatest lessons.

Keep your shoes shined.

Pass the Ketchup

I often wonder how something simple can be kept a secret, but that just seems to be the way things work: only a small percentage of people ever decide to learn what they need to in order to create the life that they have always wanted, and only a small percentage of those who learn actually apply it to their lives.

So remember the old proverb, "To know and not to do is not to know." My hope for you is that you learn and then consciously try to implement the habit that I call "Pass the Ketchup."

Let me tell you a little bit about the person who shared it with me many years ago. Most of us are lucky to have many friends in our lives, but it's been said that you are extra lucky in life if you have one true friend. Here's an interesting question to ask yourself about your friends to see whether or not you think about them in the same way that I think about my friend Morgan: If you were in need of help, you probably have a friend or two that you could call for help. But let me ask you this: If you were being detained by a group of terrorists in a foreign country, do you have a friend that you could call? A friend who would help you with bail money, ransom, or do whatever it takes, no matter what? I have such a friend. His name is Morgan, and I can promise you that he'd be on the first plane and he'd even bring his checkbook.

I've known Morgan for over three decades now. We've been together through thick and thin, through many very profitable business ventures, but also through hardships. We get together as often as we can and spend a lot of time talking about our lives and our plans for the future. It was during one of these conversations that Morgan shared his story with me.

We were talking about life and business, as we often do, but during this conversation, Morgan started talking about his grandpa. He was very close to him when he was growing up and they spent a lot of time together. In fact, they regularly had breakfast or lunch together on Saturdays.

Morgan told me that his grandpa had only an eighth-grade education, but that he had taught classes for many years on sales and marketing at the University of Minnesota. He was very goal-oriented and success-minded. He took great pleasure in helping his grandson learn the secrets to having a successful life.

One particular Saturday, Morgan and his grandpa ordered cheeseburgers and fries for lunch. When the meal arrived, Morgan grabbed the ketchup and quickly put some on his fries while also managing to splash some on his shirt. Once his fries were covered in ketchup, he started eating them. Then he started on his cheeseburger. But all of a sudden, Morgan noticed something. His grandpa wasn't eating. In fact, he was just staring back at him with a weird look on his face.

When Morgan asked what was wrong, his grandfather said, "You didn't pass me the ketchup."

Morgan was confused by this statement. "But Grandpa, you never asked me to pass the ketchup."

His grandpa said, "We've eaten together many times and you know I love ketchup when I have a cheeseburger and fries. Isn't that true?"

"Yes, of course," Morgan replied.

"Do you want to be successful in life?"

Morgan nodded.

"Then you need to learn to pass the ketchup before people ask for it."

Morgan didn't fully understand the power of what his grandpa was teaching him, but as the years went by, it became more and more clear.

In fact, over the course of his life, Morgan has made a point in both in his personal life and his professional life to anticipate the needs of others and to take action in advance. This habit, learned over lunch from his grandfather, has stood at the center of all of the success he has ever experienced in his life.

As he told me this story, I realized why I was drawn to Morgan in the first place. True friends understand how to pass the ketchup—how to think about others and not just themselves. I had appreciated this quality in Morgan for many years, but now I understood where it came from and that it was an important principle in achieving success. After Morgan shared this little story with me, it became evident to me why he had been so successful over so many years: He passes the ketchup. I discovered that this principle defines who and what you become in life.

This story made a great impact on me, and it is a part of how I have become successful. It helped me to recognize, strengthen, and nurture this habit in myself. In fact, after telling me this story, Morgan said to me, "Dave, you always pass the ketchup. It's just a part of who you are. It's as natural as breathing in and breathing out for you."

It's true—I do live my life passing the ketchup. This simple but thoughtful habit has shaped my life. But I also realized where so many challenges in my life had come from. Inevitably, when a deal hadn't worked out well, it was almost always a situation where I had chosen to do business or get involved with someone who didn't pass the ketchup; someone whose inner dialog was all about them; someone with no recognition of the importance of working together as a team and looking out for one another.

It was no accident that Morgan and I had been drawn to one another and had become such good business associates and great friends. Morgan and I pass the ketchup, and it has allowed us both to create extraordinary lives.

The motivational speaker Zig Ziglar is well known for saying, "You can have anything you want in life if you'll just help enough other people get what they want."

It's true. If you focus on providing great service, you will find that great rewards start chasing you. It's the way the world operates —or maybe it's more accurate to say it's the way the world operates when we put the secret to work. Because if you don't focus on serving others, you'll probably become very disillusioned by the fact that people won't serve you.

Never sit in front of the fireplace asking for heat. That won't work. If you want heat, build a great fire and you'll have all the warmth that you need. The only catch is that you have to act first. *It has to start with you.* Sitting and waiting in front of a fireplace and asking for heat isn't a wise approach, just like wishing others would treat you a certain way or help you with your goals isn't a formula for success unless you learn to put others first. If you want heat, build a fire and light a match, and the magic can begin. Focus on serving and watch what happens. Ask yourself how you can best serve others, and start doing it. The rewards will take care of themselves. That part is automatic.

So start passing the ketchup in your life, and watch what happens. I promise that it will transform every area of your life.

Thank you for passing the ketchup.

The Man on the Airplane

You never know who you're going to sit next to when you fly first class to Los Angeles. Who knows, perhaps you'll be seated next to a movie star, an athlete, maybe an entertainment mogul. Not that I was hoping for any particular seating arrangement this time. When I was flying out to LA for my first keynote speaking engagement, I was completely focused on reviewing my notes and being prepared to speak. But I found myself focused instead on the man seated next to me.

He was wearing suspenders and a little cap. His cane was resting between his legs. Over the course of our discussion I learned he had led an interesting life as a journalist and a world traveler. But he was also an 87-year-old man who was obviously in need of a personal nurse. I couldn't understand for the life of me why he was traveling alone in his condition.

I have to say, even after he'd shared his perfectly interesting life story, the thought that kept recurring was "Why me?" Despite this, I found myself spending the entire flight assisting my neighbor. I helped him with his meal. I wiped his chin. When nature called, I took him to the restroom. When I realized he needed help with his suspenders and then his zipper... well, I assisted him then, too. I did not necessarily *want* to help this man, but it was the right thing to do. I found myself doing it automatically, even though some of my thoughts had a different attitude about the situation.

The reason behind my act of kindness was simple: I want to do what is right. One of my core values is that I treat others how I would like to be treated myself. It's been a very successful business strategy. Like attracts like, and I work with lots of good people. It's an easy thing to say, and sometimes it's not very difficult to walk the walk. Doing what was right for the man on the airplane, however, was not as easy. It took patience, compassion, and humor.

The next day, I was giving an entrepreneurial coaching talk to a group of business professionals. I was talking about the value of doing what is right. During the middle of my talk, a gentleman stood up in the middle of the room and said to the crowd, "I want everyone here to know that this guy actually does what he says. Yesterday, I was on a flight with Dave and I saw him assist an elderly man throughout the entire flight." I was shocked! This participant was on the same flight, sitting a few rows back, watching the whole time that I was fumbling through my act of kindness.

Lessons are presented to you throughout your life. Do what most people don't do: Look at your lessons, learn from them, and then use them to create your future. A lifetime of success is achieved incrementally, one day at a time. Your daily habits define who you are and how your life will be played out. If you want to change, begin by changing your habits. Consciously increase the healthy habits that will get you where you want to be, and try to minimize the negative habits.

Human nature is most comfortable when lounging around and complaining. It is always easier to fall back into your old habits than to work on replacing them with new ones.

When you're trying to live a life that is congruent with your values and trying to replace bad habits with good ones, you'll find it takes a lot more energy to do what is right than what is convenient. Keep this in mind in order to maintain a healthy perspective as you gain the strength within you to have the patience and grace to stick to what you know is right.

Besides, you never really know when you're being watched.

"Can't You Just Lie to Me a Little Bit?"

When you're visualizing in the morning what you want the rest of your day to be like, you may take for granted that as an element of many other parts of your day, you want people to believe you when you tell them something. If you're being dishonest with yourself you are less authoritative, even when you're telling the truth to others. They can tell that something "just doesn't add up." Deep down you know it, too, and it undermines your confidence. You can't tell the truth as authoritatively or persuasively when you're deceiving yourself about other things.

Being honest with myself and being authentic are two of my core values, and there are countless reasons to practice these habits. But the fact that self-deception will damage your credibility is a simple and concrete reason that illustrates why you have to be brutally honest with yourself about who you are, who you want to be, and what you need to do to get there. Sometimes, believing one or two lies that you're telling yourself instead of accepting an unpleasant truth is holding you back from being in touch with reality. This makes it difficult to get your bearings and get back on track.

As soon as you can be honest with yourself you're suddenly back in touch with reality, able to be authentic and to progress in your desired direction.

When you have a conversation where you're able to ask for the truth and to hear it, without being in denial, getting upset, or putting the person who says it "in the penalty box," you're having what I call "an adult conversation."

One of my favorite illustrations of this came from a CEO that I was coaching. He was having trouble leading his team. After talking with him, the issues became clear: No matter what we were talking about, he insisted that his way was the best way. When you finally got a chance to speak, he'd appear to listen, but it felt as though he was just going through the motions, analyzing you as an object more than listening to what you were saying, and the whole time you couldn't help but feel like you were annoying him.

The problem he was discussing came down to a lack of likability, and I told him so.

"What?" he said.

"You're not all that likable. It's no big deal, you can work on it." He was alarmed by this, but I wouldn't be helping him if I avoided the issue. I had to be honest with him in order to get him to be honest with himself.

"You asked me to help you, and I'm helping you. Did you want me to lie to you?"

"Well, yeah! Can't you just lie to me a little bit?" he asked, cracking a smile.

I smiled, too. "See, now that was likable."

Everything changed after that. He was able to see all the excuses he had been making. He was able to see what was actually true. We worked on writing out the new habits he'd be developing and the old ones he'd be abandoning in order to work on his likability. I told him to not only be honest with himself, but to also get some outside perspective about areas that need attention by seeking out further adult conversations with people he loves and who love him. As he started mapping out how to work on his likability, he could address other challenges without feeling the need to deny them. He was able to admit that he had been dishonest with himself about his health and fitness. He resolved to lose thirty pounds and made a plan to do so.

I still see him, and he always reminds me of that session. When I think about it, I'm struck by how his being honest about wishing I would avoid telling him an unpleasant truth was all the honesty it took to start an adult conversation and to start the process of being honest with himself and making the decision to change what needed to be changed.

Often people make excuses in order to avoid an adult conversation that would make them address unpleasant truths. I like to say that life is about decisions, so you'd better make good ones. Obviously, you should make good decisions as often as possible, but when you don't make good decisions, don't compound and prolong the problem by making excuses.

When you make a decision, you are choosing a plan of action. Every action has consequences, even if that action is doing nothing. If you're right, you reap the benefits. If you're wrong, you'll have to deal with the consequences. A series of adult conversations must take place—even if you only have to answer to yourself. There are plenty of questions to ask yourself and others, information to gather and analyze, and plans to make to recover and make adjustments.

There's nothing about the process that having an excuse will change, so skip the step of avoiding the truth. Your ego, your picture of yourself, has served you well up to this point in life, but when it's time to be brutally honest, you can't avoid reality just to spare your ego. Being able to put your ego aside for a moment in order to make the changes you need to make is central to the habit of being honest with yourself and seeking out adult conversations.

There are steps to take toward positive change, no matter what the situation is. The first step is always to "get real," accept reality, and take inventory of the truth.

This is the power of getting into the habit of seeking out adult conversations—once you are able to see the power of being confronted with the need to change, of being brutally honest with yourself and making decisions and plans based on reality instead of your idea of yourself, you will find yourself able to be more authentic and make better decisions in the future—all thanks to being honest about what's really going on and not lying to yourself.

Not even a little bit.

Life's Defining Moments

What is it that finally enables people to change? Why is it that some people become endlessly stuck in life while others break free to reach new levels of success and happiness?

I believe that the answer lies in a single word. A word that has the power to change anything and everything. A simple word we use every day but seldom really think about.

The word is "decision."

It's true that we make many small decisions every day, but this story is about a type of decision that comes into focus in what I like to call a defining moment.

Can you think of a time in your life when something happened that changed your life in a major way? When a situation presented itself that required you to take a different look at an old situation and make a new decision? The kind of decision that you couldn't go back on and would forever change your life?

You can probably think of one or two of these of decisions, and most of us will have a handful of these defining moments as we travel through life: moments like taking a specific job, getting married, or having a child.

The only problem I see with the idea of defining moments is that for most of us, we let them happen rather than setting up the conditions to make them happen. We'll talk more about this later. For now, let me share one of my defining moments.

My youngest daughter, Michelle, began to get involved with alcohol and drugs when she was a teenager. For a few years, I was unaware of the problem because she hid it very well. But as she got older, the signs began appearing and the attempts to heal the problem proved ineffective. In fact, by the time she was nineteen years old she had an incident where she had flatlined for almost a full minute.

If you've ever tried to help someone that has a drug or alcohol problem, you know how challenging it can be, especially if it's your own child. The defining moment that came from this occurred when I was called to the hospital because Michelle had attempted suicide. I can't imagine a pain that cuts as deep as when your child's life is in danger. It's the kind of problem that will bring almost anyone to their knees. In this case, my daughter pulled through the suicide attempt, which gave me the opportunity to talk with her about her life and what she was feeling.

We actually had a great conversation that day. It's a conversation that I will never forget, and it's a conversation that created a defining moment for both Michelle and me.

At one point in the conversation, I said to Michelle, "Honey, how's all this working for you?"

Michelle said, "Not well."

I said, "I'll do anything that I can to help you, but we have to start by telling the truth about the situation."

Michelle said, "Well, Dad, I can get real if you can get real."

I was shocked by this comment, given the circumstances. I said to Michelle, "What do you mean, *me* get real?"

Without hesitating, Michelle said, "You and Mom."

"What do you mean?"

"You guys should have been divorced years ago."

In that moment, everything changed for both of us. I realized that I was living a lie, and Michelle realized that her life was out of control. It was a defining moment that neither one of us will ever forget.

That moment changed our lives because we both made a decision to change. Michelle decided that she had to get help, and I decided that I had to do the necessary work with my wife to determine whether or not we should be together. Ultimately, we did get divorced not that long after this incident occurred, but the change really happened in the instant that I reminded myself of the importance of telling the truth and making real decisions.

Now let's get to the important part. What decision do you need to make?

Like so many defining moments, the one that I just described happened without my planning or forethought. But I've learned that defining moments don't always have to be that way. We can decide to change things at any moment in time. It's true that the actual change might take some time to transpire, but the truth of the matter is that once you've really decided, you are living a new reality even if you have to work through the process to make the changes.

So how about creating a defining moment today? How about deciding to change something that's been holding you back? Perhaps it's not as radical as getting a divorce, especially since trying to save a marriage should always be the top priority. But what if no matter what you do, it just doesn't work? What if the person you are with just isn't compatible with you and you're not compatible with them? I did everything I could think of to make my marriage work, but the truth of the matter was that no matter what I did, it wasn't going to work, and it was making me unhappy.

What I've since learned is that the divorce has actually been good for my now ex-wife as well, because it has enabled her to get on with her life and her priorities. After Michelle met her defining moment, she went on to start the hard work of recovery. She just celebrated four years of sobriety and is thriving like never before.

Ask yourself: What do I need to do to make my life work for me? How can I enjoy my life more and help other people in the process? What gifts have I been given that only I can share with the world?

What's most important is to realize that you can change your life, and you can do it today if you really want to. All that's needed is a decision—a decision that means you will never go back to the old way.

Make one of those decisions today and you will have created a brand-new defining moment in your life.

Goalie Days

A goalie must have one overriding quality—
he must want to be a goalie.
- Emile Francis

Decisions have consequences. If we don't make them for ourselves, who does? Some decisions are tougher than others. Some are subtle. Some are forced on you from the outside, and you can never be completely sure what the outcome will be. One of the most important decisions in my life happened right as I was becoming an adult, at that time in a person's life when decisions set things into motion for the rest of their life. It was the crossroads where I first stepped onto the path I'm still on today, and where I first encountered "the path not taken" I had heard so much about.

When you're good at something, it can be difficult to step back and realize that for all of your ability and success in that particular arena, it isn't the right ability to build your life around. For me it was sports. I was good at sports, and they were instrumental for me in making it through my childhood; with all of the trouble I had at home, the sense of success that I was allowed to earn in sports, as well as the opportunity to be coached and led to an attitude of achievement, were priceless.

I was a good goalie. My high school hockey coach worked with me as much as he could, but at the end of the day I was self-taught and relied on my natural athleticism to make up for the gaps in my training. Apart from my coach, I was the only person motivating myself. My mother encouraged me, but she couldn't help with the sports stuff. I didn't have a dad that encouraged me or taught me anything—other than what not to do. I was trying to process life decisions on my own. I started with a bang as a tenth-grader on the varsity team and got noticed immediately. As a junior and senior, some real opportunities were presented to me.

When Mel Pearson, a former player for the Minnesota Fighting Saints, became the coach and manager for the Flin Flon Bombers, he invited me to try out for the team. Flin Flon, Manitoba is 500 miles north of Winnipeg, which meant it was 1000 miles from my home in Minneapolis. I went up and competed against the best players I had ever shared the ice with. There were 114 players trying out, including 14 goalies. Of all the competitors, only two were American: myself and Rick, a hockey buddy of mine from Minnesota, a defenseman. The Canadian style of play was more competitive and aggressive than either of us was used to. I had to take it all in and rise to the occasion in order to hold my own. I was getting the hang of it and had started to earn the respect of the other competitors when, after about a week, Rick decided it wasn't for him.

Two weeks later I was called into Mel's office. They had cut the goalies down to just four, and they were going to make the final cuts. Mel said I was on the team if I wanted it, but he wanted me to think about it. So I went for a long walk to think by myself. I thought about it: being 1000 miles from home, playing hockey in this tiny town in Canada. I thought about the offers in front of me: The Bombers, The Olympics. I thought about what it would be like to live the lifestyle of an athlete. Then I thought about everything back in Minneapolis. I thought about family life, going to college, starting a career. For all the excitement offered by the prospect of Pearson's offer, there was something about it that I knew wasn't for me. I decided to go back to Minneapolis, enroll in college, and marry my high school sweetheart.

Over the years I've thought about how I took the path I did, and what my life might look like had I chosen to stay in Manitoba to play hockey. It can get a little overwhelming when you think like that: What if the past had been different? I could imagine having gone all the way to the pros, eventually becoming a coach, or even an owner of an NHL team. The possibilities were there once. The fantasies are nice, but that's all they are. The past wasn't different, and I'm glad. What I see now is that I made the right decision.

I was good at hockey. Pearson's invitation proved that. Moreover, sports had made me able to make it through my childhood, but they were not going to see me through the rest of my life. I wanted something else. I wasn't sure at the time, but I realize now that this was the root of my reluctance to take the position on the team. Hockey, and sports in general, had served me well, but it was time to move on. I took the confidence that came from all the success and accomplishment I had earned and began my journey to discover who I really was, who I wanted to be, what my values were, and how to live the life I wanted to.

It's another example of how a single decision can totally change your life. If I hadn't gone back to Minneapolis, I wouldn't have married the woman I did and I wouldn't have the children I have. I wouldn't be in the business I'm in. I wouldn't have met many of the wonderful people that I have in my life now.

But I did, and I know what decisions got me here. I know which path I didn't take, and I feel great about the path I did.

Can you remember experiences like this, where paths split in your life? Do you need to flip the way you look at some of your experiences so that you can enjoy where you are now, and create the path you want for the future?

Trophies

One of the biggest influences on my character as a coach was my coach in the Little League Majors, Coach Butner. I mentioned before that I started in the league as a ten-year-old. What I didn't mention was that when I was ten, I was six feet tall. Apparently this seemed unfair to some of the parents of the opposing teams. I hit a home run once, and a woman was watching while working the concession stand with my mother. She was suspicious and said, "You can't tell me that huge kid is ten." My mom said, "Yeah, I can. He's my son."

My team won that season. Naturally, we were excited about this. However, Coach Butner told the team that there was a "problem with the budget" and we wouldn't be getting trophies to commemorate our victory. What it really came down to was that the parents of the kids on the losing teams didn't want their kids to feel bad seeing the winners get trophies.

Coach Butner didn't go along with their thinking. He went out and purchased trophies for us at his own expense and presented them to us. The trophies were only about five or six inches tall, but I kept mine and displayed it in my office for many years until it was lost in a move. I loved to look at that trophy. It symbolized one of my life's great lessons, and I would often remember Coach Butner and his example of acknowledging the winners.

Later in my life, after becoming a parent and becoming involved in youth sports activities, I gained more perspective on those parents who hadn't wanted their children to feel distraught over losing. I was able to understand where those parents were coming from. But I still say that robbing the winners of recognition and the pride that comes from it is the wrong technique, and the fearful attitude toward failure that is represented by the parents not wanting to reward the winners is a problem in and of itself.

While understandable on the surface, it comes from an unchecked belief that failure is a hazard that must be avoided, as opposed to something that happens when you compete but still have lessons to learn and abilities to develop.

The point of recognizing success isn't to punish failure. It is to incentivize those that didn't win to take stock, focus on improving, try harder, and try to win next time.

What those parents didn't connect to the situation was that they were preventing their children from learning this very important lesson: the value of improving yourself in order to reach a reward.

When success isn't recognized and rewarded, it can demotivate and frustrate some of the most capable performers in any field. So, especially in business, I love a results-based structure. When people go the extra mile, when they "pass the ketchup," and make a difference, I believe that it's the right thing to do to reward them.

I know that the members of my business teams as individuals are excited to make my companies successful. But they don't get out of bed and say, "How can I make Dave LaRue more money today." No. I believe that they're doing it for themselves, for their families—for the rewards that come with earning success. Because I believe in results-based pay and rewarding achievement, they are able to earn more for themselves by earning more for the company, and everyone wins when that happens.

It's important and necessary to learn from failure in order to prevent it in the future. But it's equally necessary to reward success. If you punish failure but don't reward success, you make an enemy out of failure but offer no consolation in achievement.

How do you feel about failure, and how does this cause you to deal with failure in yourself and others? Are you doing all you can to reward the winners? When you really understand failure and success, you'll see that trophies reward the winners and motivate others to compete to be winners in the future.

Give the winners trophies.

The Teacher Appears

When a total stranger spares none of the details in sharing the biggest problems and challenges in their life with you, and they hug you goodbye with tears in their eyes, saying that talking to you was the most important two hours in their life, it's obviously something special to them. And it's special to me.

There was a time before I had fully embraced my talent for coaching. I realized I needed to start paying attention to it when within the space of three days I had two encounters on airplanes that helped me to understand it.

On a flight from Minneapolis to Los Angeles, the man seated next to me had been on the phone when he boarded the plane, and he had distractedly put his bag on my seat. When he moved it, I thanked him. He finished his call, apologized, and introduced himself. He started telling me his story and the purpose of his trip, and the challenges before him.

His final destination was Auckland, New Zealand. He had just been hired as a marketing VP for a company there to help them enter the American market. He was going into meetings with many people he'd be meeting for the first time: the owners, the manufacturing team, the marketing team, and so on. I spent the next four hours strategizing with him, laying out plans and objectives for his trip. Then we talked about his US marketing plan so he would be prepared for his meetings and the questions that would be asked.

When we landed in Los Angeles, Guy didn't know what to say or do. He shook my hand and held it for longer than normal. He said he didn't know how to thank me. I said without hesitation, "Don't treat your new strategies the way I treated my talent for coaching."

He didn't know what I meant. I said, "I just gave you a multimillion-dollar strategy for free. Make sure you treat it as though you had to pay a million dollars for it. Then you'll be sure to put it to good use, as though you had to get your money's worth out of it." I was beginning to see that I had to value my ability for what it was worth and not take it for granted just because it was something I did naturally.

Only a few days later, I was given another opportunity to learn the same lesson. This time, I was sitting next to a man who worked for a major property management firm. We were flying into St. Louis from Minneapolis. He told me he was flying out to St Louis for a promotion.

"That's great," I said.

"No, not really," he said. "My family is in Minneapolis, and I'm going through a divorce." He reflected for a moment and said, "You know, I wanted to take an earlier flight, but I took this one instead."

I was having my own moment of reflection and said, "The reason is probably because you needed to sit by me. You know what they say: 'The teacher will appear when the student is willing.'"

We got to talking and I realized that he cared about his daughters but hadn't considered how the move would affect his relationship with them.

"If you're living in St Louis, what do you think the probability is that you'll be a part of their life?" I said.

"Well, kind of low."

"Low or not at all? What about when their mom's life changes, or when you meet someone else and start getting more commitments in St. Louis. How are you going to do both?" He realized he was rushing to a make decision that he didn't realize there were alternatives to.

"Imagine the future," I said. "When your girls are going to the prom, do you want to be there?" I asked. "Do you want to be part of the excitement? Or in just a couple years, imagine they're at their dance recital. Do you want to be there?" He did. I said, "Let's make a plan and write it out."

We did, and after we were done he shook his head and said, "This is amazing."

"It's amazing if you do something with it. Otherwise, it's just free advice."

I reflected on the teaching and learning that happened between us. His lesson was that he had two beautiful daughters and that he wanted desperately to be in their lives, but he was making this decision to relocate based solely on his career. I gave him the confidence to realize that he had more choices than he was aware of.

My lesson was that I just touched the life of a hurting man, and it meant a lot to me to be able to do that.

These encounters made me realize how much I liked helping people get on the right path. I had quoted the line, "The teacher appears when the student is willing" to the man headed to St. Louis, but what I didn't really realize until a little later was that this situation had taught me that it's also true that for someone who wants to coach and lead others, the *student* appears when the *teacher* is willing. I already knew that I was good at coaching and leading, and that I got a lot out of doing it. But these encounters caused me to embrace the fact that it's more than a role I play—it's a part of who I am. The more I could accept this, the more I found myself getting the chance to do what I love to do.

When did you finally embrace your talents and make a commitment to use them as much as possible?

Not Everyone Will Be Coming With You

I often talk about how crucial it is to drop bad habits and adopt good ones, about how once you discover what your values are, how important it is to live in accordance with them, and about how, ultimately, life is about decisions.

I had made the decision to stop playing hockey and instead get married and start a family. I decided to work for and learn from Bob Nyrop. Because of these decisions, as well as all the effort I had put into developing myself through applying all of the reading and learning I had done up to that point, my life was very different from the one I had imagined to be waiting for me on the other side of my childhood. I had found values that I wanted to live by and was living by them. I was surrounded by people and opportunities that were positive and constructive. Success was a present reality for me.

The past wasn't done talking to me, though.

Thanksgiving is about different things to different people. Family, food, and football are what most people think about when they think about the holiday, but gathering all of the family into a common space can also be the cause of some pretty big upsets: sibling rivalry flare-ups, airing of dirty family laundry, political arguments, and all sorts of things can cause a traumatic scene around the television or the table. This story doesn't have those kinds of fireworks, but it stands in my mind as one day when several lessons were learned in a short amount of time.

I loved my wife's family. Her mom, Gladys, and her dad, Bob, as well as her aunts and uncles, were all very special to me. They were an inspiration to me and a big part of my life. When our family was young, we would have both sides of the family together for the holidays. My mom, my aunt and uncle, my sister and her husband would join me, Cindy, and the kids, as well as Cindy's mom, dad, aunt, and uncle to celebrate the holidays. I thought it was nice to spend the holiday together as one big family, but I learned that not everyone agreed with that. When I was coming back inside from the deck, I overheard my family complaining about the spread we had laid out for them, rolling their eyes, and making fun of my mother-in-law and Aunt Ruby.

I couldn't believe what I was hearing. I was upset. I was disgusted. I didn't know what to say. At that point in my life, I hadn't learned how to have conversations like this yet. All I could say was "What are you doing?" It was the best I could come up with to try to express my disappointment, disapproval, sadness, and embarrassment at being confronted in the same room with the difference between where I came from and what I aspired to be. Thankfully, Cindy's side of the family was never aware of the incident.

I was still in the process of becoming what I wanted to be, and the culture shock I experienced from witnessing this conflict in values was painful. But it reinforced my decision to break the cycle. It crystallized for me that it's impossible to change people who don't want to change, and who are unaware of the fact that some change would do them good.

I knew that I had made changes and gone a different way from the values of the family I came from. What I hadn't realized is that I had wrongly assumed that the rest of my family would see the value in the changes I had made, and not only be happy for me, but make the same changes for themselves. It was painful to find out how wrong I was.

At the time, all I knew was that my family's behavior was not right. After I had some time to process, this incident helped me formulate my philosophy of choices, what I now sum up by saying "life is about decisions." I also realized that I was captain of my ship and master of my soul. I redoubled my efforts to engage the success principles that I had studied since I was a teenager. I realized that I was responsible for my bigger future and that of my family.

I saw in my father-in-law the antidote to the attitude toward fatherhood that my own father had exemplified. He showed me how a loving dad puts his family first. He taught me that I could show my own children many ways to approach life and help them decide which type of person they would rather become: an eye-roller or a doer.

Another way I learned to look at the value differences in this story is to look at whether your focus is on achievement or on justification. Either way you go, you will only see more of what you've decided to look for. When you focus on justification—excuses—you will always see more of them.

However, when you're focused on achievement you see all of the possibilities available to you. You think in terms of what needs to happen in order to reach your end goal. You're motivated by the energy and opportunity you will get from your accomplishments.

Many people grow up in a family with a justification model and the mental habits that come from that perspective. I know I did. But after I had made the decision to focus on achievement and live my life that way, I couldn't bring myself to abide by the excuse-based values of eye-rollers, even out of a sense of obligation to the family I had grown up with.

So that's the lesson of that Thanksgiving. I learned that the changes I made had affected only me. They *could* affect only me. I was the only one who had wanted to change, and I was the only one who had. It was a powerful moment when I realized this, and I'm thankful for the lesson, even though it was sad to know that they wouldn't be coming along with me for the ride.

Giving

One of the aspects of success that you learn about after you get there is figuring out how to use your success to be a positive force of change in the world, the society you're a part of, and the community you live in. It's something that I truly enjoy, and there are a few ways that I go about doing it.

When it comes to giving, I don't subscribe to the "shotgun" approach. I give to the causes that truly matter to me rather than giving smaller amounts to many causes that I care less about. This is because I believe it's important to be consistent with your values. Give if you really care, not because it looks good.

There are other ways to give. My talent for coaching grants me an opportunity to do what I love and make a difference at the same time. When my daughter was attending FIDM Fashion Institute in Los Angeles, one of her instructors invited me to speak to students in their "Career Skills" class. It was supposed to be only a thirty-minute talk, but after I arrived her teacher asked if I would just go ahead and talk for the whole three hours of the class period. I was a little surprised, and I guess I could have been frustrated that they didn't give me any notice, but I wasn't. In fact, I was honored to have been given the opportunity.

The class was made up of students who were all headed into the world with big ideas. They were both excited and afraid, going through lots of different emotions and thoughts. I heard their thoughts, their questions, their dreams, and learned their values. I had them take inventory of the support they got from their teachers, family, and friends, and take a moment to appreciate all the people who had helped them get to where they were at that moment. Then I helped them link up their values with their goals. I noticed a lot of the students really got it, and I got a lot of satisfaction out of that.

What I felt like I really did was give these young people permission to take charge of their journeys and to not carry the guilt of choosing a career that gives them joy and satisfaction, and not to worry about what other people would think or say about it. Many of these students had a lot of passion for particular causes and beliefs, so the last thing I told them was to focus on making profitable companies before anything else. I made sure they understood that you could do both—you could be successful in business and in giving, but there is a definite order to things: the profitable business creates the opportunity to give and really make a difference.

That piece of advice is close to my heart. One of the ways I feel that I give the most is through my businesses. As I continue to embrace the joy of creating and growing my businesses, I've discovered that one of the experiences I value most as an entrepreneur is creating opportunities for others. By building successful businesses that are great places to work, I create opportunities for people to have great careers that allow them to do something they love and make a living at it. The income that they earn and the success that they achieve allow each one of them to get involved in their communities and make a difference in the lives of their families, friends, and members of their community in unique ways according to their individual values.

Entrepreneurs and business owners create so many opportunities for so many people in the world by making the plans and taking the risks that they do. It's something that moves me. I admire these risk-takers and I love what they do for our world. If you're one of them, make sure you take the time to appreciate the power you have to make the world an even better place. It's a priceless perk that comes with being a successful entrepreneur, and one of the things that fuels my passion for creating and running successful businesses.

Think of all the ways you're able to give as an entrepreneur, and take a moment to appreciate how valuable the opportunity is. And if someone in your life, perhaps your husband or wife, gives you the opportunity to contribute to the causes they care about, be sure to thank them. It's a beautiful thing!

Understudy to the Prodigal Son

It's one thing to hear a parable and grasp a personal meaning, another to hear a story and be told what it means, and another thing altogether when you realize years later that you've played a major part in a real-life re-enactment. When I was twenty-four years old I took part in a version of the parable of the prodigal son, and the experience provided me with many important lessons that have shaped my values ever since.

So here is the story of how as a young man I charged off toward glory, only to have to return home with my tail between my legs, and how, by taking accountability for my mistakes and making amends, I was shown grace. I also learned the value of always doing the right thing, the power of forgiveness, and the reason why you need to reward people for their good work.

I was working for my father-in-law, Bob. He had a 50/50 partner in the firm, and that partner had a son. The son —I'll call him George —was heir apparent to the firm, but he was also almost forty years old and no longer content to work for his father. I was twenty-four and had been working for my father-in-law for the better part of seven years. Where George was impatient for change, I was enthusiastic about working my way up in the world, and had always dreamed of running my own business. I had been reading and learning and doing everything I could in order to make this happen for myself. I was excited by the idea—maybe this was my moment, at long last! Sure, I was young, I thought, but maybe my dedication to improving myself was paying off faster than I expected. It could happen.

I was thinking all kinds of thoughts, but the bottom line was that George was able to speak to my ambition and convince me to go along with his idea to attempt to talk his father and my father-in-law into a buyout plan.

When we presented our plan, what we thought of as a "power play," it was, surprisingly to us, a no-go. The old guys didn't think it was the right time to pass over the reins. We tried to push past their reluctance; no dice. The old guys had two words for us: "Good Luck."

Just like that, George and I were on our own.

We made the best of it. We seized the day. George had his talents, and I had mine. I made sales calls and George ran the office. Sales were good, but slow. One day, a little over a year later, I looked up and realized that I couldn't go on like this. I was twenty-six with a young family. The break with my father-in-law had put a great deal of strain on my wife and her mother. I was barely making any money, and I had a $24,000 bank note hanging over my head. I needed to get out and I had nowhere to go. Except back to my father-in-law.

I prepared myself to crawl back on my hands and knees, to start from scratch and earn his trust again, to admit that I had done something that caused a lot of pain to everyone and had not profited from it. I was ready to admit I had been utterly, sorrowfully wrong.

And I did.

And instead of making me grovel, instead of putting me in the penalty box, or being too hurt to talk to me, my father-in-law took me back. He helped me clean up the mess of my failed venture. He gave me my job back. He took over the bank note. I told him I would pay him back and he told me he knew I would.

George had a totally different experience. He continued to run the business we had started and made it successful, but George and his father couldn't speak to each other for years afterward. I don't know much about the reasons why, but I don't think they ever fully recovered from the upset. Eventually, before his father died, they started speaking again, but they had lost so much valuable time that they could have spent together.

Because I was so young there are questions I never asked, and because of this there are answers that I'll never have about why things went how they did. I know that my father-in-law believed in me, and I know he was able to see that if I was willing to come back to him and take ownership of my actions, that I would make it up to him. Had I been oblivious, or too proud to admit my mistake, I know that things would not have gone like they did. Beyond that, I'll never get the chance to know what his thoughts were. I'd love to know, but unfortunately that's impossible now.

What I am able to reflect on was what my frame of mind was at the time. I was working hard and doing a good job, and something in me bristled when, instead of being offered bonuses based on my performance, I was gifted a certain amount at the end of the year, unrelated to my efforts. I had a hunger for recognition of my results, and I wasn't getting it. This is the personal reason why I believe in results-based pay: I know what it feels like to want recognition in kind.

This episode went on to inform another one of my values in business, which is creating entrepreneurial companies, not companies that create entrepreneurs. By making a place where great people can work hard and apply their unique abilities passionately in order to be rewarded for their outstanding achievements, ambitious, talented people will happily stay and contribute to an incredible team instead of having to strike out on their own in order to get the recognition they deserve.

The business lessons are valuable to me, but the greatest lessons I learned from this episode were about taking responsibility for my actions, doing the right thing, and what it is to receive grace. Bob never rubbed my mistake in my face. He never brought it up again. We could talk about it; there wasn't any denial about it, but he didn't see it necessary to bring up something we were already aware of. He gave me a chance to redeem myself and I did. I worked for him harder than ever. His investment of faith in me paid off for both of us. We were able to move on, heal, and build on the break. I made him millions of dollars, and he went on to teach me all of the priceless lessons he did about business and life.

And now that he's gone, the story of this episode still has lessons of its own to teach me. This is how I know the value of seeing your life as a series of stories.

Making a timeline or mapping out a series of cause-and-effect relationships has its own use. Analyzing your life this way has great value and is a crucial part of the process of assessing reality, charting a course, and making changes.

The difference between facts and stories is the difference between remembering something and understanding it. When I talk about the stories of your life, I'm talking about the difference between being able to account for your time and remember your life, and being able to learn from your experiences and relationships and truly understand their value and their meaning.

Stories have lessons. Like jokes, we bury wisdom in them: observations about life and people, lessons, truth. Looking at the stories of your life opens up the possibility that you can learn deeply from your experiences. What's more is that with stories you can share your experience with others in such a way that they can get to know you and your values, while taking their own lessons from those stories as they listen and see parallels in their own life.

When you see the stories of your life as important, you can become aware of the fact that the moments that become stories are the moments when you were truly present and in conversation with life. Even when you're unable to immediately understand what life is trying to tell you, the story is there, waiting to share its lessons with you, just like any teacher—when the student is willing.

While so far I've explained how telling the stories of your life makes it possible to extract lessons from the past, it's important that you know that one of the most joyful aspects of focusing on stories has to do with your present and your future. Once you decide to reflect on your life as a series of stories, you start to look forward to having the next new experience, knowing that it will become another story to have and to share. You will seek out people and situations that are worth talking about later. When you encounter challenges, when you're faced with a dilemma, when something catastrophic happens that tries and tests your character, a part of you will be able to look at the big picture and start to look for the meaning of the experience. You will truly be able to learn from your experiences and use what you learn to make the decisions that shape your life.

What a tremendous value in such a simple decision.

Afterword

I hope you enjoyed these stories. I enjoy the life they have come from and the life I'm living each day as I collect more of them. For me, there is nothing better than relating the story of a great experience and extracting both the positive lessons and negative lessons from the experience and transforming them into opportunities to learn and improve. Whenever a flight gets delayed or something doesn't go exactly according to plan, I think, "This will be a story. I can't wait to tell it."

Don't wait to tell your stories. Don't wait to find the punchlines and lessons and hints at meaning in the tales of your life. Seek out your stories, reflect on them, share them, treasure their lessons, and use them to chart the path toward the life you want.

Ultimately, it's up to you to decide what your stories will be. If you're not surrounded by the kinds of people and opportunities that lead to the kinds of stories you want to tell, make the changes you need to find and attract them. If you feel that your role in the stories of your life doesn't reflect the values that you believe in or the person you want to be, change your habits in order to act congruently. The story of your life is the document of your life's work, and taking control of it is something you can't just leave to chance. It's as simple as making the decision and doing what needs to be done.

The legacy you leave may take many forms, but largely it will be in the stories you leave for others—the actions you took that represented your values, the way you touched their lives, the lessons you helped them learn, the opportunities you created for them. The stories of your life are proof of your actions and the effect they had on the world and the people in your life. They are a special kind of currency that buys priceless things that money can't. At the end of the day that's why I called this book *Live to Tell Your Story*: it's a short sentence that sums up so many of the lessons that I've learned and found so much joy in sharing. In learning and sharing the lessons and stories of your own life you can have that joy, too.

Live to tell your story.

D.L. July, 2012

www.ingramcontent.com/pod-product-compliance
Lightning Source LLC
Chambersburg PA
CBHW060503110426
42738CB00055B/2606